Presented to

By

Date

Cover illustration and all lyric excerpts from the collection,

A Child's Gift of Lullabyes

Text copyright © 1993 by Ideals Publishing Corporation
Illustrations copyright © 1993 by Someday Baby, Inc.

Cover illustration copyright © 1987 by Someday Baby, Inc.
Lyrics copyright © 1986 by J. Aaron Brown & Associates, Inc.
Nashville, Tennessee 37212
Used by permission.

All rights reserved. No part of this publication may be reproduced or transmitted in any form or by any means, electronic or mechanical, including photocopy, recording, or any information storage and retrieval system, without permission in writing from the publisher.

Published by Ideals Publishing Corporation
Nashville, Tennessee 37214

Printed and bound in the United States of America.

ISBN 0-8249-8619-9 (book)
ISBN 0-8249-7586-3 (set)

The display type is set in Belwe Light.
The text type is set in Souvenir Gothic.
The lyrics are set in Freehand 591.

Color separations by Rayson Films.
Printed and bound by Worzalla Publishing.

A Child's Gift of Lullabyes is a registered trademark of Someday Baby, Inc.

Baby Days & Lullabye Nights

Illustrations by Teresa B. Ragland

Ideals Publishing Corporation • Nashville, Tennessee

Here Comes Baby

Name

Date of birth

Day

Time of birth

Place of birth

Mother

Father

Doctor

Attendants

Special moments

photo space

All About Baby

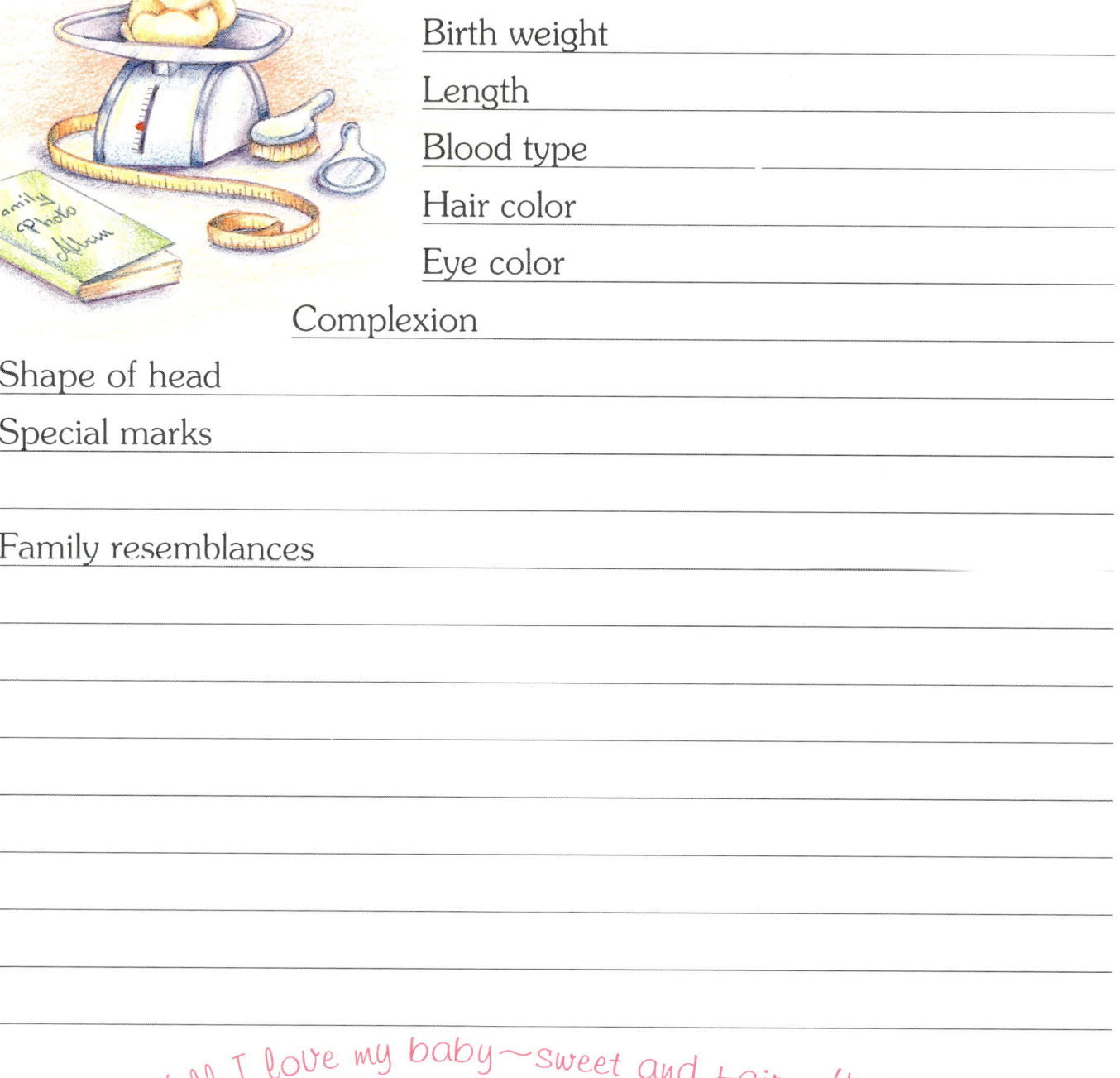

Birth weight _____

Length _____

Blood type _____

Hair color _____

Eye color _____

Complexion _____

Shape of head _____

Special marks _____

_____

Family resemblances _____

_____

_____

_____

_____

_____

_____

Well I love my baby~sweet and fair~You've got the sky in yo

The Story of Baby's Name

First name

Middle name

Last name

es~the sun in your hair~I rock you to sleep most every night

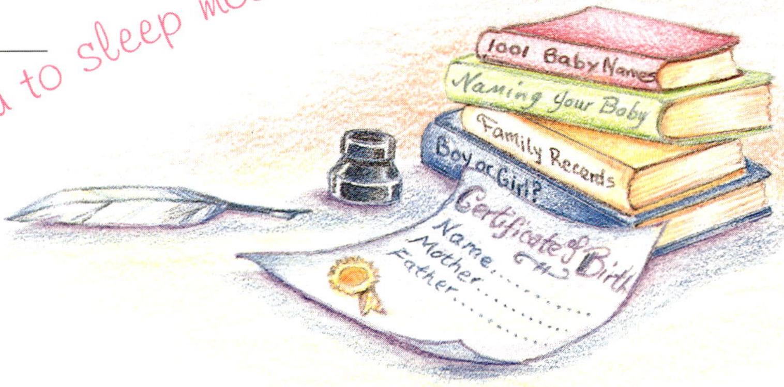

1001 Baby Names
Naming your Baby
Family Records
Boy or Girl?
Certificate of Birth
Name
Mother
Father

photo space

Baby's Family Tree

_____
Baby

_____   _____
Mother   Father

_____
Brothers and sisters

_____   _____
Grandmother   Grandmother

_____   _____
Grandfather   Grandfather

Our Thoughts About Baby

Mother

Father

Brothers and sisters

Grandparents

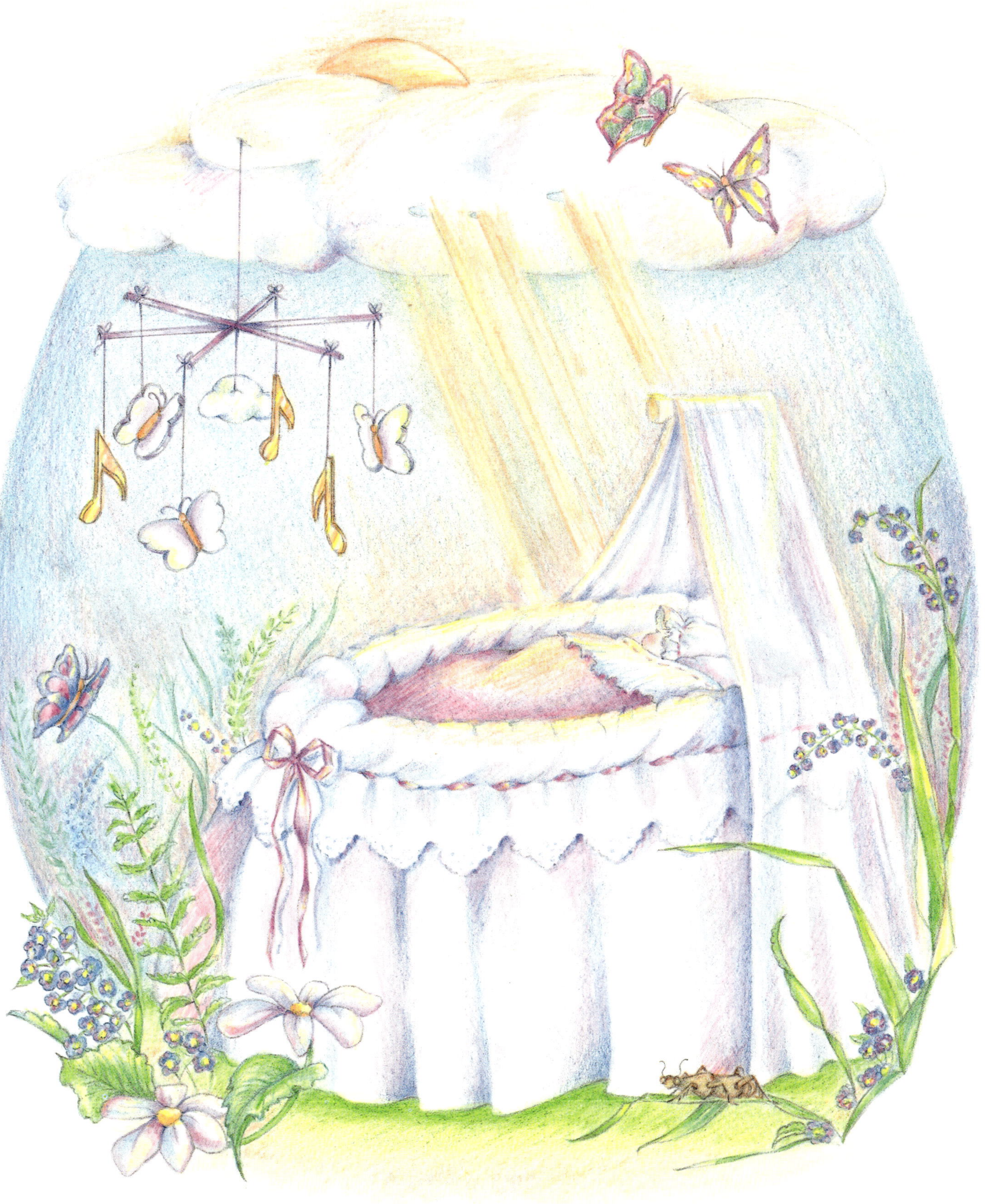

paste birth announcement here

The World Around Us

World news

National news

Local news

Prominent people

Clothing styles

Current prices

Baby Comes Home

Date _____

Weather _____

_____

Baby's attire _____

_____

Address _____

_____

_____

Baby's room _____

_____

_____

First day at home _____

_____

_____

_____

_____

_____

_____

photo space

Visitors and Gifts

Favorite Notes and Cards

Visitors and Gifts

Heaven has given to me~the loveliest gift that ca[n]

Baby's First Ceremony

Date

Place

Baby's attire

Sponsors

Officiated by

Guests

The ceremony

~And I cherish the sight~of those eyes closing tight

Going to the Doctor

Age

Doctor

Weight   Height

Percentile

Baby's behavior

Parents' feelings

Diagnostic tests

Doctor's comments

Keeping Baby Healthy

Series Dates   Booster Dates

DPT _____   _____

_____   _____

_____   _____

HIB _____   _____

_____   _____

_____   _____

Polio _____ _____

_____   _____

_____

PPD/Tine _____

MMR _____   _____

Allergies

_____

_____

_____

_____

_____

Watching Baby Grow

Age				Height				Weight				Percentile

Baby Days & Lullabye Nights

At three months

Feeding time _____

_____

Naptime _____

Playtime _____

_____

_____

At six months

Feeding time _____

Naptime _____

Playtime _____

_____

_____

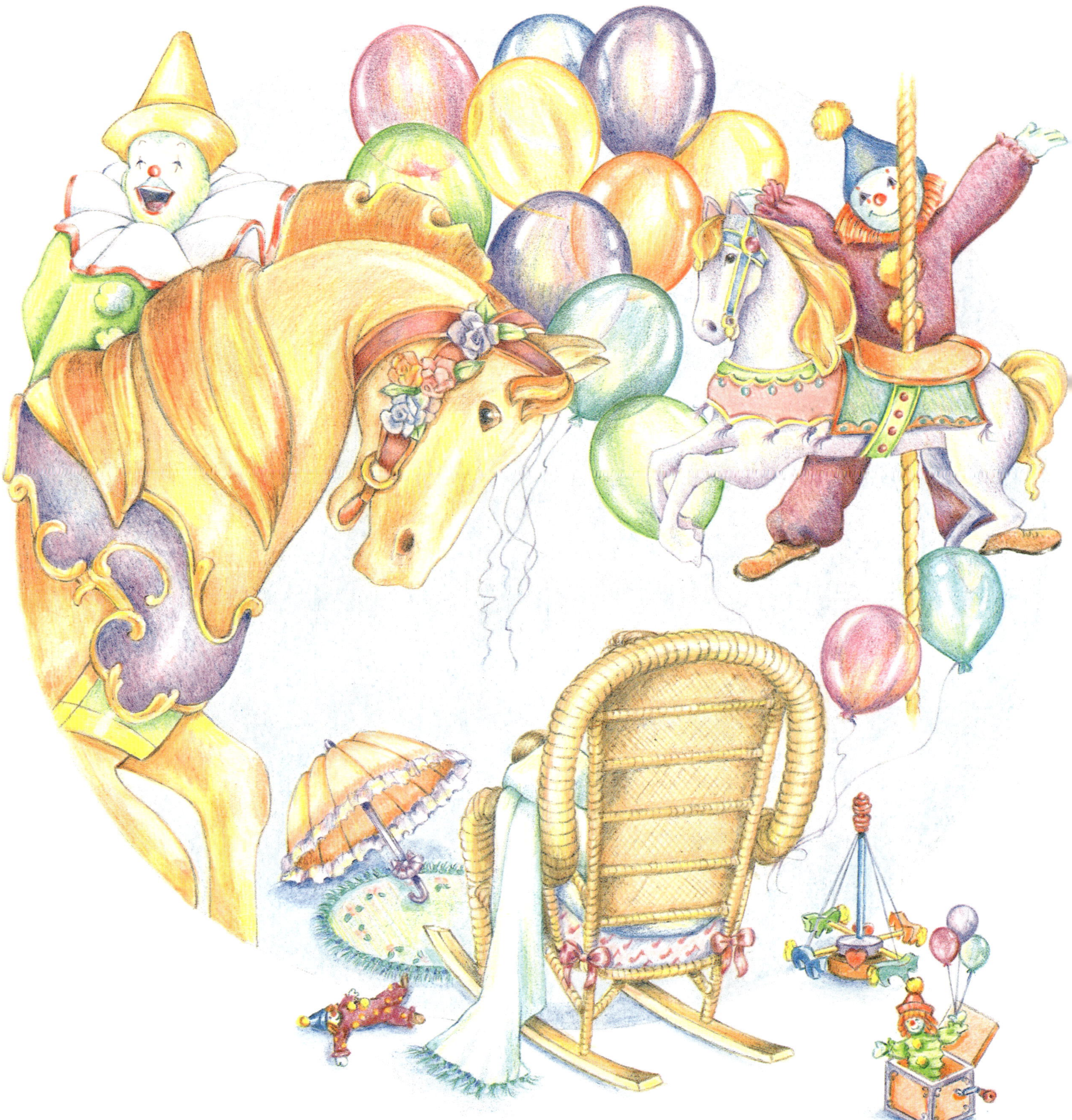

Baby Days & Lullabye Nights

At nine months

Feeding time
_____
_____

Naptime
_____
_____

Playtime
_____
_____
_____
_____

At twelve months

Feeding time
_____
_____

Naptime
_____
_____

Playtime
_____
_____
_____
_____

Baby's First Christmas

Baby's age

Place of celebration

Weather

Family and guests

Presents in stocking

Presents under tree

Baby's reaction

photo space

Christmas Comes Again

Age two

Age three

. . . and Again

Age four

Age five

Baby's Stepping Out

Date

Place

Weather

Baby's attire

Baby's behavior

Parents' feelings

As quick as a wink~the morning u

Big Moments

Smiles   Age
_____
_____

Rolls over   Age
_____
_____

Laughs out loud   Age
_____
_____

Has a tooth   Age
_____
_____

Sleeps all night   Age
_____
_____

ak~Soon we'll be there~tomorrow we'll go to the fair

. . . and Little Steps

Sits up _____ Age _____

_____

_____

Waves bye-bye _____ Age _____

_____

_____

Crawls _____ Age _____

_____

_____

Speaks a word _____ Age _____

_____

_____

Gives a kiss _____ Age _____

_____

_____

. . . in the Life

Gets into mischief   Age

Plays peek-a-boo   Age

Stands up alone   Age

Takes a step   Age

Plays patty-cake   Age

. . . of Baby

Blows a kiss   Age
_____
_____

Dances   Age
_____
_____

Drinks from a cup   Age
_____
_____

Uses a spoon   Age
_____
_____

Says "please" and "thank-you"   Age
_____
_____

Baby's First Masterpiece

paste baby's artwork here

photo space

Holiday Baby

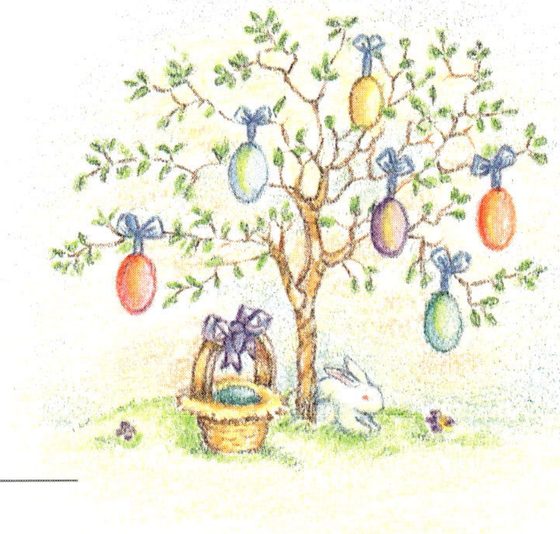

Easter

Baby's Easter attire

Easter basket for baby

Special moments

Thanksgiving

Place of gathering

What baby ate

Special moments

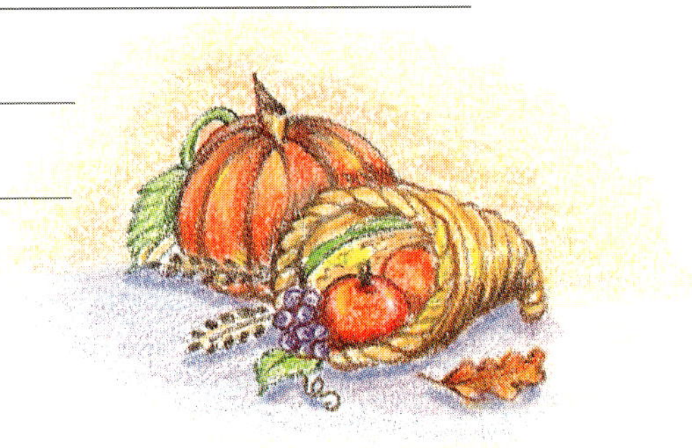

Baby's Playmates

Playmate's name _____

Baby's age _____ Playmate's age _____

Favorite activities _____

_____

_____

Playmate's name _____

Baby's age _____ Playmate's age _____

Favorite activities _____

_____

_____

Playmate's name _____

Baby's age _____ Playmate's age _____

Favorite activities _____

_____

Look at Teddy~he's so tired~he's been playing very hard~Litt

What Baby Enjoys

Places _____ Age _____

_____

_____

People _____ Age _____

_____

_____

Foods _____ Age _____

_____

_____

Songs _____ Age _____

_____

...ddy needs his sleep—but bears aren't good at counting sheep

Games _____ Age _____

_____

_____

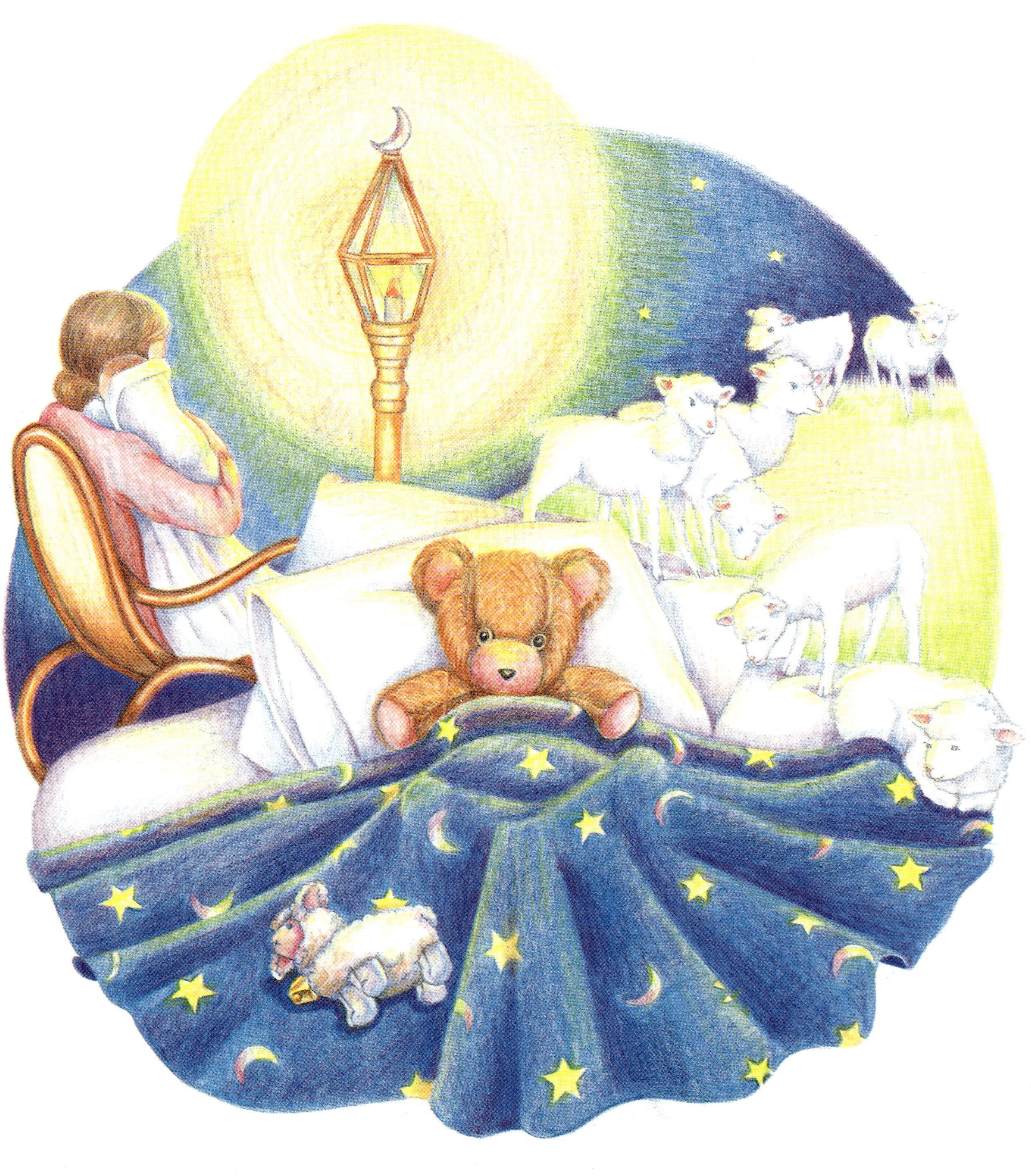

Baby's Treasures

Favorite book _____ Age _____

_____

_____

_____

Favorite sleepytime toy _____ Age _____

_____

_____

_____

Favorite lullaby _____ Age _____

_____

_____

_____

Favorite article of clothing _____ Age _____

_____

_____

_____

Baby's First Birthday

Baby's cake _____

Place _____

Baby's attire _____

Family and friends _____
_____
_____
_____

Gifts _____
_____
_____
_____

Baby's reactions _____
_____
_____
_____
_____

photo space

Baby Grows Up

Second birthday

_____
_____
_____
_____
_____
_____
_____

Sunbeams fall from up above~chasing clouds away with love

Third birthday

_____
_____
_____
_____
_____
_____
_____
_____

Baby Grows Up

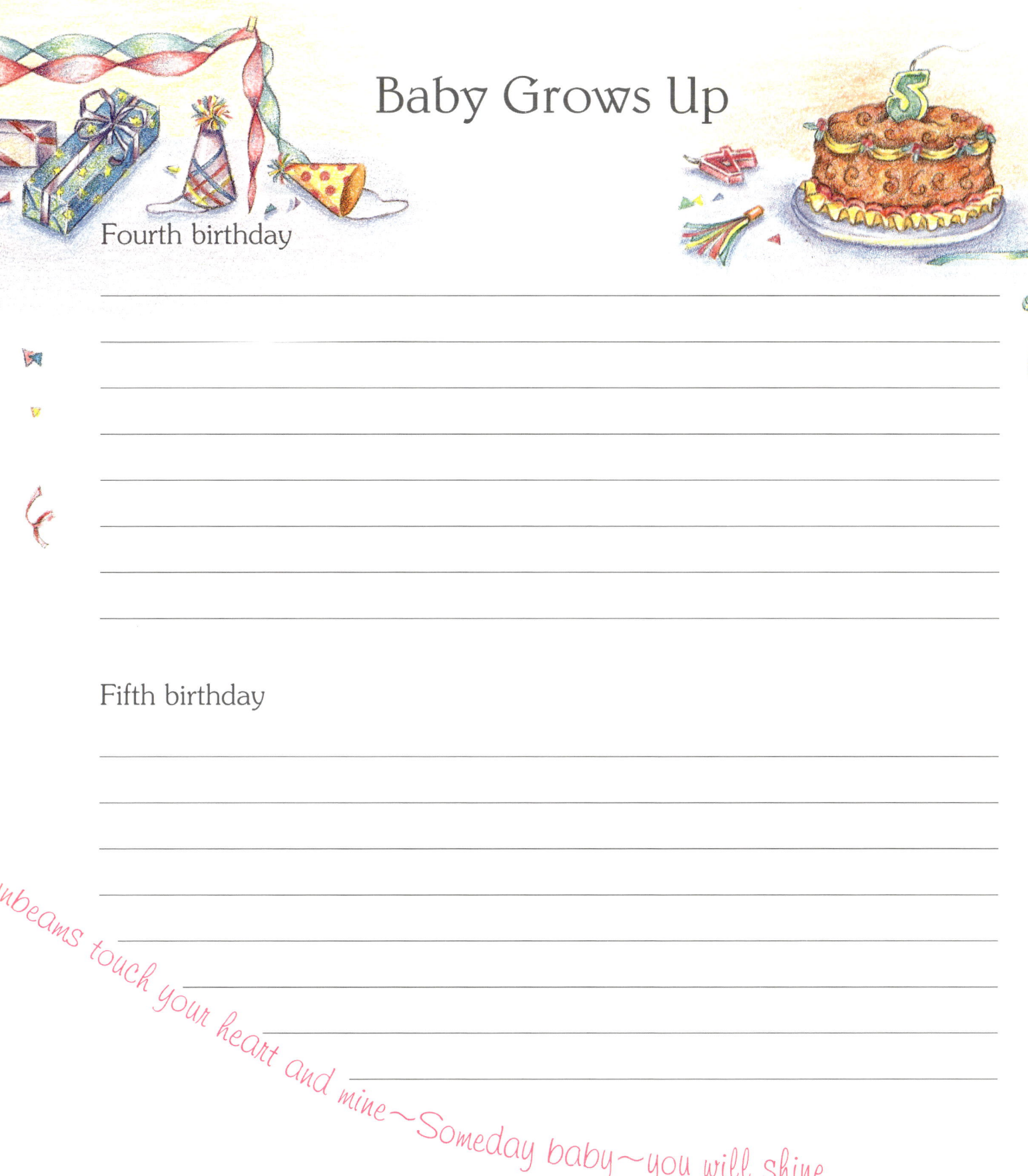

Fourth birthday

Fifth birthday

Sunbeams touch your heart and mine~Someday baby~you will shine

Off to School

Date _____

School _____

Level _____

Teacher _____

First day of school _____
_____
_____

Child's reaction _____
_____
_____

Parent's feelings _____
_____
_____

Off to School

Favorite school activities
_____
_____
_____
_____

School friends
_____
_____
_____
_____

Report card grades
_____
_____
_____
_____

photo space